FAIR TRADING

Fair Trading

Published by: Diwan Press Ltd.
6 Terrace Walk,
Norwich
NR1 3JD
UK
Website: www.diwanpress.com
E-mail: info@diwanpress.com

Author: Dr. Asadullah Yate
Typesetting and cover design: Abdassamad Clarke

A catalogue record of this book is available from the British Library.

ISBN-13: 978-1-908892-33-1
(paperback)

Printed and bound by: Lightning Source

FAIR TRADING

DR. ASADULLAH YATE

Diwan (+) Press

Classical and Contemporary Books on Islam and Sufism

CONTENTS

IN THE NAME OF ALLAH THE ALL-
MERCIFUL, THE MOST MERCIFUL

FAIR TRADING

Fair trading (***'adl***) in the market-place is based on trust. The establishment of healthy trade is an act of worship, modelled upon the trading practice of the Messenger of Allah, may the peace and blessings of Allah be upon him.

As a principle, any exchange of goods is permitted as long as it does not involve:

a. forbidden commodities (e.g. wine, pig)

b. usury (any increase without corresponding counter-value)

c. uncertainty (e.g. sale of wheat before it is harvested, or fish before they are caught)

d. fraud (e.g. charging higher prices to travellers unaware of local prices)

e. extortion (e.g. manipulation of market conditions, monopoly, monopsomy)

CUSTOMARY PRACTICE

Fair trading is also based on a community's understanding of the value of things, that is, their customary practice (*'urf*); the local community must be left to make its own evaluation of goods. It cannot be an evaluation imposed from above or from outside.

USURY

Usury is the most pernicious destroyer of equity in the market-place and is the gateway to social imbalance and oppression and the proliferation of other malpractices. Previous generations took great pains to identify those transactions in which elements of usury had been introduced wittingly or unwittingly.

However innocuous a usurious transaction may seem, there is always an underlying element of gain for one party at the expense of loss for the other. Those engaged in such activity, Ibn Rushd[1] states, "pay out money and receive more back without performing any deed or assuming any liability".

Ibn Rushd insisted on the social importance of this question. "It is obvious from the *shari'ah*

---

1   Ibn Rushd, the author of *Bidayat al-Mujtahid.*

that the reason for prohibiting usury is to prevent the fraud that it entails. Justice in transactions consists in close approximation and equivalence [between the goods exchanged]".

MEANS OF EXCHANGE (CURRENCIES)

Currencies exist in any trading situation. Ibn Rushd indicates the purpose of currency: "Since it is difficult to equate the values of things whose natures are different, *dinars* and *dirhams* are used to price them". Here gold coins (*dinars*) and silver coins (*dirhams*) and similar non-perishable, easily quantifiable commodities with intrinsic value, not bank-notes, are referred to.

It is acceptable for those in authority to standardise currency to ensure its reliability, e.g. by issuing assayed and weighed gold and silver coins. It is against market equity for the authorities or any cartel, such as the banks, to monopolise the means of exchange. This enables the authorities, whether of bank or state, to debase the coinage (which is a hidden, and forbidden, taxation!) which is usurious because the authorities can contract debts at one value in real terms and pay them back at other values.

The creation of monopoly in the means of exchange also allows the appearance of *fiat* money – currency, based on faith, with no intrinsic worth, such as paper or electronic credits, whose value is imposed politically. This involves the fraudulent exchange of real assets for worthless tokens and facilitates the usurious manipulation of devaluation, inflation and deflation.

THE SALE OF COMMODITIES

In order to prevent usury, you can only exchange commodities sold by weight and measure i.e. **staple foodstuffs**, **gold** and **silver**, for the same type of commodity e.g. minted gold for unminted gold or good dates for poor dates, when you exchange equal weight for equal weight, measure for measure, with no deferral of payment. Ibn Rushd explains it thus: "Given that there are no radical differences between specimens of the same type, when their uses are approximately the same, and the person in possession of one type has no pressing need to exchange it for another of the same type, except by way of extravagance, equity is obtainable only on the basis of equivalence in terms of weight and measure". In other words it is permitted, albeit regarded as an 'extravagance', to exchange *patna* rice for *basmati*, but only as long as the weight of the *patna* equals that of the *basmati*.

FORBIDDEN SALES IN COMMODITIES

Ibn Rushd lists eight examples of sales, each of which demonstrates how usury enters into sales of commodities.

(1) "Give me respite [from repayment of a debt or payment for goods bought on credit] and I will increase [the amount to be paid]". (In other words the borrower or purchaser, addressing the lender or seller, says "Give me more time to pay the debt and I will pay you back more").

(2) A sale with forbidden disparity. (This refers to staples, storable foodstuffs, gold and silver which cannot be exchanged 'with each other' with disparity: thus an exchange of 1 gold coin for 10 silver coins is permitted but an exchange of two pounds of poor quality dates for one pound of good quality dates is not. If good quality dates are required, the poor quality dates must be sold and good quality dates bought with the proceeds).

(3) A sale with forbidden delayed payment. (This refers to gold in exchange for silver, dates in exchange for raisins, or wheat etc., etc., which although of different types cannot be exchanged with each other when payment of one of the two is not immediate).

(4) A sale combined with a loan. (All contracts which are composed of more than one transaction are forbidden).

(5) A sale of gold and merchandise for gold. (This is because, in effect, gold is being sold for gold with disparity – the merchandise only obscuring the transaction).

(6) The sale known as 'reduce the amount in return for immediate settlement'. (This is a kind of usury in which the borrower who has agreed to pay back money by a certain date offers to pay a smaller amount before this date – now known as discounting of bills or factoring of debts).

(7) The sale of foodstuff which has not yet been received in full [by the seller]. (Actual possession must be taken of all foodstuffs before their resale).

(8) A sale combined with a money change. (Again, this is a transaction in which the equivalence demanded of any money change is obscured by the accompanying sale and is also two transactions in one contract).

Ibn Rushd cites "the protection of wealth and prevention of squandering" as Malik's explanation for the prohibition of usury. He also mentions Ibn al-Majishun's explanation as "preservation of property (*hiyata al-amwal*) meaning that fraud should be prevented".

The term "usury" has a much wider definition than that of [modern] English law: usury, in effect, can occur in almost any transaction; thus pure sales, barter transactions, money exchanges, speculation, the leasing of land for a share of its produce, control through monopoly etc. are all subject to the prohibition of usury if unjustified increase accrues to one party.

THE ELIMINATION OF PARASITICAL THIRD PARTIES

What is significant for us is that parasitical third parties, state interference, commercial taxes and devious practices have no place in the Muslim trading world: there can be no money lenders, no bankers, no speculators, no stock exchanges, no promissory notes, no bonds, no lotteries. Traders must be free to operate within a basically healthy arena in which the pillars of sound trade are in place, namely free access to gold and silver as currency and the right to choose any means of exchange, unfettered by the tyranny of paper, plastic or computerised money, free of the monopoly of the banking system which governs all financial and political transactions today.

In the concluding remarks to the *Bidaya al-Mujtahid* Ibn Rushd points out that the underlying rationale of all transactions regulated by the law is the establishment and maintenance of human virtues, in this case that of justice. The way of the Muslims, the *shari'ah*, is composed of various behavioural patterns or *sunnas*. The prohibition of usury, risk and speculation are among the *sunnas* which "relate to the pursuit of justice and the avoidance of oppression: these are the kinds of *sunna* which demand equity in financial matters (*al-'adl fi'l-amwal*) and justice amongst people."

TRADE

Traders move goods from a place, where these goods are in abundance, to another where there is a market for them. The trader expends energy in his going out to find suitable goods, in securing a reasonable price for them, in transporting and guarding them safely, and finally in selling them to a second party. Usurers, however, rent out money, which by its nature is only utilised by natural communities as a means of exchange, and merely wait for its return with increase. They produce nothing, do not contribute any work and do not incur any risk. They are parasitical third parties who borrow from one source at one rate and lend to another at a higher rate thus preventing direct contact between investors and entrepreneurs. The most sophisticated form of usury is the establishment of 'national banks' which gather up a country's gold and silver, prohibit its use by the people, print paper money – of which they have the monopoly – in its stead and then raise or decrease its 'value' (by devaluation, inflation or exchange-rate adjustments) to create speculation and the opportunity for vast profit.

Trade is generated from the face to face meeting of men who do not negotiate with any third party, be it in the guise of state tax regulations, customs tariffs, bankers, brokers, insurers or specialists in 'international' law. A trader's handshake or his word is enough to seal a **contract**.

CONTRACTS

A contract is an act of trust between two people. Its reality extends beyond the material exchange of two commodities. A trader knows that his reputation for honest dealing is the key to swift and uncomplicated exchanges. Written contracts are drawn up whenever the exchange of goods or payment is delayed and the two parties see this to be of mutual benefit – when agreed delivery dates and precise measurements of commodities to be supplied in the future, for example, might otherwise be forgotten. Likewise witnesses may be signatories to a contract if their presence facilitates trust between the two parties.

In general, a contract – that is an offer and an acceptance and the obligation [to supply or pay for something] – is binding upon the parties when the buyer accepts the seller's offer, before the two parties separate. **When the buyer takes possession of the goods he usually accepts liability for them**. There is, however, a **warranty period**, during which the buyer may return the goods to the seller and recover his payment if he discovers a defect in the goods. This is as long as the two parties have not agreed upon a waiver of this warranty (*bara'a*) during their meeting. The seller may not normally impose any condition on the buyer restricting the latter's ownership of the goods.

FORMS OF CONTRACT

The Prophet, may the peace and blessings of Allah be upon him, sanctioned **qirad investments** which exclude any usurious third party: by it the investor (*rabb al-mal*) makes over a certain sum of money (in gold or silver) to an 'agent' (*al-'amil*). The agent uses these funds to trade and pays back the capital plus a previously-agreed percentage of the profits to the investor when the goods bought with the funds have been sold. The increased return on the initial investment is equitable as it is a loan which incurs risk for both parties: if the agent makes a loss (on the investment and on his time and work) the investor will also make a loss.

PARTNERSHIP

Partnership (*shirka*) likewise excludes usurers. By it, two or more parties come together and contribute equal shares of money, goods, equipment and work (*shirka al-amwal*), and then divide the profit between themselves equally. If the contribution from one partner (of either money, goods, equipment or work) is greater than the other partner, equity must be established by a division of the profits which is in proportion to this disparity. Equity may also be established in a partnership by one partner

11

contributing all the equipment, for example, and the other contributing all the goods, as long as the rental value of the equipment and the profit-potential of the goods is approximately the same. Partnerships based solely on persons' work (*shirka al-abdan*, i.e. when two cobblers come together and 'share' the same customers) must be located under one roof. Each partner is liable for delivery of orders taken by the other. When partnerships are based on money, each partner is free to buy and sell with the 'pooled' money of the partnership (that is a ***mufawada partnership of mutual delegation***); when trading out of their localities, partnership funds may be used for travel expenses and maintenance of each partner's family. It is, however, permitted to restrict the use of the 'pooled' resources by a mutual agreement to only buy and sell with both partners' knowledge.

SHIRKA FI'L-BAY'

A ***shirka fi'l-ba'y*** contract is one in which one party says to the other: 'Make me an equal partner in this article belonging to you on condition that I sell it for you'. In effect what happens in this transaction is that the article is transferred to the first party without payment of money. It is equitable, however as the first party has become a partner in the article and pays for it by undertaking to sell it (in this respect it is not dissimilar to a contract of hire whereby the owner 'hires' the services of another party and pays for this hire by making him a partner in the goods). When he does sell it, he pays back half of the original value of the article to the second party together with half of the profit realised by their partnership. The 'owner' of the goods may fix a minimum price or the expected profit margin for the article which the other will sell.

MURABAHA

A *murabaha* **sale** is one in which a trader goes to another city and states prior to a deal that he is selling a commodity for such and such an amount above his cost price. This transaction is permitted as it is essentially the same as buying and selling: it is equitable as both parties are legitimate traders who both agree on the nature and quality of the subject matter of sale and their profit margin prior to any dealing. It is based on the first party's trust that the other party will always only add on, for example, 10% profit for himself on top of the price of the goods and his expenses incurred in procuring and delivering them.

SALAM

In any sale/exchange, payment and the taking delivery of the goods is normally simultaneous. A ***salam* contract** is a form of sale on delayed terms in which the money (or anything used in payment) may be paid first and the goods delivered at a later date. This is to permit the making of a contract for goods which are in another country or only available, for example, on the market day of the following month. The precise date of delivery must be stipulated. The commodities exchanged must be different to each other in kind or in use, and must not involve the exchange of food for food or gold for silver. The salam contract does not stipulate that a specific object will be delivered at such and such a date but rather stipulates the *type* of object, like a horse or a sword. A ***nasi'a*** contract is similar except the money is paid later. It is not permitted, however, that *both* payment and delivery of the thing paid for are delayed. In any sale, be the payment or delivery of goods immediate or delayed, transfer of ownership is effected at the time of the deal (i.e. immediately the offer of the first partner is accepted by the first).

IJARA

A **rental contract** (*kira'*, *ijara*) is one in which one party, the leaseholder (***al-mustajir***), pays for the temporary use of a house, beast, or piece of equipment. The contract must stipulate the hire-charge, the period of hire and the location in which the thing hired is to be used. The owner (***al-malik***) of the rented article is liable for any damage to the article. Similar to this are contracts of hire regarding persons engaged to work for a daily, weekly or monthly wage (***ijara***) or to complete a specific job for a specific reward in a time which is not specified (***ju'al***). Although it is permitted to 'hire' someone to buy you something it is not permitted for you to ask him to use his own money on the understanding that you will pay him back later.

MARKETS

The Amir sets aside areas as markets in which the people may come to sell their goods and in which no place may be reserved and upon whose trade no taxes may be levied. The stalls are of a non-permanent nature, erected merely for the protection of the traders and the goods from the weather. They are there so that those who want goods from artisans, farmers and agents may buy them from them. People set them up at times of harvest, on the arrival of caravans and for a variety of other seasonal and social reasons. They are not a prelude to the establishment of fixed, structured shops, grocers, engrossers, wholesalers or 'supermarkets'. These latter only hoard and monopolise commodities in order to control and manipulate prices. Markets, when they reach this stage of 'development', become a barrier to free exchange for those who wish to buy and sell at a modest level. All such practices (known as **engrossing** and **regrating** in English law) were outlawed by edict until the introduction of foreign 'Banking' law (i.e. the law of the moneylenders and hoarders) at the beginning of the 18th century. Outside of that obligatory market, which is a *waqf*, there may be fixed shops' – which are in fact 'stores', 'almacenes' in the original sense of places of storage from where goods are taken to the market – for if the market is truly free of taxes then the goods on sale there are naturally going to be the cheapest.

CARAVANS

A **caravan** is a group of traders, *qirad* agents, partners or artisans who travel together to establish new markets or take part in existing markets outside their home cities in order to buy and sell. Their travelling together affords the protection of a **company** of men, and protection from the dangers of the open road. They should not have to pay any taxes in the establishment of these markets. They only require the permission of the local Amir. It is not permitted for people to go out to meet the caravan before it has arrived in a town in order to buy goods wholesale and at a lower price than the goods would otherwise have fetched on the open market (**forestalling**).

ZAKAT

We must recognise the obligation of paying **zakat-**tax on wealth to the Amir as well as and at the same time as establishing free markets. Payment of the **zakat** purifies and increases the wealth generated from trading, confirms traders **allegiance** to their Amir and ensures the distribution of surplus wealth to the poor, the needy, those fighting in the way of Allah and for justice, and other categories of persons.

Commenting on Allah's words: *"That which is given [as zakat-tax] is for the poor, the needy, those who work for this [zakat], for those whose hearts might come closer [to Allah], for slaves, for debtors, and in the way of Allah and for the traveller: [this is] an obligation from Allah, and Allah is the Knower, the Wise."* (Sura *at-Tawba*, *ayat* 60), Ibn Juzayy in his *Qawanin* says: "As for 'those who work for this [*zakat*]', they are the persons who collect, distribute and record it, **even if they have independent means**…. This depends upon their being just and knowledgeable of *zakat*-law.

As for 'those whose hearts might come close [to Allah]', they are the kuffar, to whom it is given in order to encourage them to Islam.

Its distribution is according to the estimation of the Amir. It is permitted to give it to only one of the eight categories of persons mentioned in the Qur'an, or to give preference to one category over another. Moreover anyone who qualifies for two of the categories has a right to two shares.

It is not to be transferred from the region in which it was collected, except when there is an excess.

The *zakat* is not to be spent on building mosques, nor on burying the dead.

It is obligatory to pay the *zakat* to the Amir if he is just."

GLOSSARY

'adl: equity, the root of this word refers to the balance obtained when the two pannier-bags on either side of a beast of burden are of equal weight.

al-'amil: the agent who works with the *qirad* investment

barter: the exchange of goods for goods, or commodity for commodity which in a normal market situation is often a more common means of exchange than goods for money.

caravan: traders who keep company with each other while they journey together to markets.

condition: any condition imposed on a contract which limits ownership of the goods is usually invalid.

contract: an offer and acceptance followed by exchange of goods and payment.

engrossing: buying up all of a commodity in order to control prices; monopoly.

forbidden commodities: those which of their nature are unclean, like pork, or those which for external reasons are not permitted, like stolen goods.

forestalling: the act of going out to meet traders before they have brought their goods on to the market.

fraud (*ghabn*): it may also be translated as 'loss' when *ghaban* enters a contract unbeknown to the two partners.

gold coins: gold and silver, and the copper or nickel coins (*fals* pl. *fulus*) used for small change, are the only kinds of 'money' acceptable in the *shari'ah*.

liability: liability for the goods usually becomes the buyer's as soon as he takes possession of them.

loan: only a loan free of any increase for the lender is permitted; loans may be made for trade but their reward is with Allah.

market: a place set aside to receive caravans, artisans and farmers who come to sell on particular days; any stalls should be of a temporary nature and not designed as stores or shops.

mufawada **partnership**: a partnership

in which each partner delegates mutual responsibility for buying and selling.

murabaha **sale**: an agreement to supply another with goods for a fixed and pre-determined profit – this would include, for example, the cost of the goods to the supplier, any expenses he incurs in their transport, and 10% profit.

option of return (*khiyar*): the right of the buyer to return goods if found to be defective after he has taken possession of them; a warranty period, usually of three days, but shorter in the case of fruit and longer in the case of a house.

partnership: an agreement by which two or more persons (equally) contribute money, goods, equipment or work and receive a profit in proportion to their contribution.

qirad **investment**: investing money with an agent-trader who returns the capital to the investor plus a previously-agreed share of the profit on completion of the buying and selling.

rabb al-mal: the person who invests the money in a qirad contract.

regrating: buying up a particular commodity to sell it again in the same or another market.

salam **contract**: whereby payment is made

after the contract and the thing paid for is received at a later date.

shirka al-abdan: a partnership based on the partners' work.

shirka al-amwal: a partnership based on the partners' contribution of gold or silver.

shirka fi'l-ba'y: the transfer at cost price of an article to another who in return becomes a partner in the ownership of the article and agrees to sell it for both of them.

taking possession: taking possession of the goods pur-chased usually marks the transfer of liability to the purchaser.

uncertainty *(gharar)*: also known as risk or alea; any contract in which the availability of goods promised cannot be guaranteed is invalidated through this element of risk.

'urf: those practices of a community which do not conflict with the *shari'ah* and which may be retained in Islam.

usury *(riba)*: literally 'increase'; in general, any unjustified increase accruing to one party to a sale; more specifically, disparity in any exchange of 'usurious foodstuffs' or gold and silver, either by way of a difference in weight or a delay in delivery of these commodities, when one of these commodities is exchanged for a commodity of the same genus.

zakat: on cash (*'ayn*)the payment of two and a half percent of one's standing wealth when it is over a threshold (*nisab*); it must be paid to the Amir or his appointed collected (*'amilina*) once a lunar year. The Amir may distribute it to any or all of the eight categories of persons mentioned by Allah in the Qur'an.

SOURCE BOOKS

The general prohibition of paper-money is explained by 'Umar Vadillo in his *Fatwa on Paper Money*. The means to effecting a transition from usurious markets to permitted 'white' markets in which there is free circulation of gold and silver is explained in his *The End of Economics*.

Descriptions of the different kinds of partnership may be found in the 'Book of Partnership' in the *Mudawwana* of Sahnun at-Tanukhi (from Ibn al-Qasim and Imam Malik). A detailed analysis of what constitute usurious, fraudulent or forbidden sales and the principles underlying the jurist's rulings may be found in the 'Book of Sales' in Ibn Rushd's *Bidaya al-Mujtahid*. The *Qawanin* of Ibn Juzayy provides briefer summaries of such sales.

THE BIRMINGHAM FAIR TRADE FAIR

Dr. Asadullah Yate prepared this booklet for the historic Birmingham Fair Trade Fair of October 1992 to which a party of Andalusian traders led by Shaykh Umar Ibrahim Vadillo came, having minted silver dirhams and gold dinars in Granada, as did a group of Muslims from Brixton, led by their amir Uthman Ibrahim-Morrison, who also brought

FAIR TRADE FAIR

TRADE WAR!

GOVERNANCE WITHOUT STATE
COMMERCE WITHOUT USURY

The Old School of Arts
496 Moseley Rd
Birmingham
on
Saturday and Sunday
24th and 25th October
1992

Contact the Murabitun
Tel: 021 449 3977/523 4264 for enquiries and stall spaces.

with them newly minted silver dirhams. The coins were accepted as payment at the Fair and this was the first time in the 20th century that genuine currency was used in trade in the British Isles.

www.ingramcontent.com/pod-product-compliance
Lightning Source LLC
Chambersburg PA
CBHW060555030426
42337CB00019B/3555